# YOUR PATRIARCHAL BLESSING

BRAD WILCOX

DESERET BOOK

SALT LAKE CITY, UTAH

TO HUGH W. NIBLEY
(1910–2005),
who helped me see patriarchal
blessings through new eyes

© 2021 The Brad and Debi Wilcox Family Trust

All rights reserved. No part of this book may be reproduced in any form or by any means without permission in writing from the publisher, Deseret Book Company, at permissions@deseretbook.com. This work is not an official publication of The Church of Jesus Christ of Latter-day Saints. The views expressed herein are the responsibility of the author and do not necessarily represent the position of the Church or of Deseret Book Company.

Deseret Book is a registered trademark of Deseret Book Company.

Visit us at deseretbook.com

ISBN 978-1-62972-921-3

Printed in the United States of America
PubLitho, Draper, UT

10  9  8  7  6  5  4  3

## THE BIG PICTURE

Our family enjoys doing puzzles. It started when the children were young and we wanted to keep them in the room listening during general conference broadcasts. Once the puzzles were finished, my wife Debi could never stand to undo them, so she glued them together and hung them in our garage. Now those walls are covered from top to bottom. That is a lot of general conference sessions!

I recall once when we started a puzzle and then lost the box with the picture on the front. We tried to finish the puzzle without it, but it became almost impossible. Without the big picture, it was hard to see how the little pieces fit together. Soon we just gave up.

Your patriarchal blessing is like the picture on the puzzle box. It helps you keep the end in mind and focus on what matters most. The big picture can keep you motivated to put the pieces together and work toward the desired outcome. Every puzzle is different, and some puzzles may be more difficult than others. You may not put your pieces together in the same sequence as the next person, but the picture on the box assures you that one day all the pieces will fit and form a finished—and beautiful—end product. Your patriarchal blessing provides inspired direction from Heavenly Father. It warns you of possible dangers and gives you personalized counsel. It points you toward your potential.

You can read of similar blessings given by Adam (see D&C 107:42) and Jacob in the Old Testament (see Genesis 49) as well as Lehi in the Book of Mormon (see 2 Nephi 4). Today, when you desire to receive a patriarchal blessing, you request an interview with your bishop, who gives you a Patriarchal Blessing Recommend. You may then contact the patriarch and set up an appointment. The correct way to address him is "Brother so-and-so" and not "Patriarch so-and-so."

Elder Neal A. Maxwell taught that within the grand plan of salvation for everyone, there is also a plan for each one. That does not mean God controls or micromanages His children. It just shows "how very long and how perfectly God has loved us and known us with our individual needs and capacities."[1]

God teaches His grand plan for everyone through scriptures and the words of living prophets. He teaches His personal plan for you in your patriarchal blessing. Your blessing is not about guarantees, but opportunities—and responsibilities. President Thomas S. Monson said, "A patriarchal blessing is a revelation to the recipient, even a white line down the middle of the road, to protect, inspire, and motivate activity and righteousness. A patriarchal blessing literally contains chapters from your book of eternal possibilities."[2]

It helps you find and fulfill your mission in life. In a world where too many worry and fret about small and insignificant things, your blessing helps you see—and rise—above. With it, you take one more step toward viewing yourself as God does and discovering the principles and perspectives that can guide you through life's trials. It helps you find the big peace and big joy that await you when you see the big picture—a big picture that encompasses this life and beyond.[3]

## YOUR LIFE MISSION

Ramon grew up near family. His best friends were his cousins. In the fields and orchards near their homes, Ramon and his cousins made huts and slept out under the stars. He loved staring at the night sky and trying to count the stars after his cousins fell asleep. The stars made him think of how many children God has. But instead of that making him feel small and insignificant, Ramon felt important and loved. He figured that surely a God with the power to create all the stars had the power to care for all His children. Ramon was grateful for the blessings of his family and the Church, and he knew that where much is given, much is required. Did he have anything to offer? He was just a normal kid living a normal life. Did God have an important work for him to do?

Why are you here on earth? Children in Primary learn that we come to earth to receive a body, be tested, gain experience, and learn to have faith. However, you could have done all that a thousand years ago. Why were you born *right now*? Like Ramon, you must realize the blessings you have been given are for a purpose greater than yourself. Something deep inside tells you "souls matter more than stars"[4] and God needs you to do important things.

Sister Wendy W. Nelson said, "The only thing that really matters is that you and I are doing exactly what we committed—even covenanted—premortally with our Heavenly Father we *would* do while we are here on earth. So, let me ask you a question: What *were you* born to do?" She then provided the answer: "Find and fulfill your mortal missions."[5]

I recall being in attendance when Stephen R. Covey spoke to a group of students at Brigham Young University. He was a highly effective Latter-day Saint author and consultant who instructed business and government leaders about how to write their personal mission statements. However, when he spoke to the BYU students, he changed his message. He told them not to *write* their mission statements, but to *discern* their personal missions.

Discernment is not just the ability to judge well, but also to seek and obtain spiritual guidance and understanding. Sometimes that awareness happens during the sacrament or in the temple. Sometimes it happens during prayer—especially when you take time to listen as well as speak. Sometimes it happens when, like Ramon, you pause long enough to look at the nighttime sky and ponder your relationship with God and the work He has for you to do. One of the greatest gifts you can receive to help you in this line-upon-line discerning process is a patriarchal blessing.

I received mine as a young teenager and—to be honest—was disappointed because it was shorter than the blessings of other family members. I figured somehow that meant I was not as important to God. I had hoped my blessing would say I was talented and a leader. It did not say any of that—at least not in the way I expected.

One day when I was in high school, some peers and I gathered at a friend's house to plan an upcoming activity. Somehow, the topic of patriarchal blessings came up, and I shared my disappointment that mine was so short. I said, "It doesn't say anything about talents or leadership or . . ."

Right then, from around the corner came my friend's father. Right in front of the group, he said, "Brad, your patriarchal blessing is not so God can tell you what you already know. It is the chance for Him to tell you what He needs you to know."

When I got home, I reread my blessing through the new lens I had been given, and my feelings changed. Suddenly, I loved my blessing—not just because it validated and reaffirmed what I hoped was the case, but also because it taught me something new. I had only read it thinking about what was important to me at the time. Now, I saw what was important to God and what needed to become more important to me. My blessing helped me start discerning my missions in life—a learning process that has continued to this day.

God sees the big picture. That is why you can trust Him when He does not always answer your prayers in the way you desire or according to your timeline.[6] In the same way, you can trust what He tells you in your patriarchal blessing. That sacred blessing—no matter its length—will help you discern, discover, and do what God desires.

President Spencer W. Kimball testified that before we came here, faithful women and men were given certain assignments and tasks. "While we do not now remember the particulars," he wrote, "this does not alter the glorious reality of what we once agreed to. You are accountable for those things which long ago were expected of you just as are those we sustain as prophets and apostles!"[7] It is time for you and me to be about our Father's business (see Luke 2:49).

## THE BEST TIME FOR YOU

Lily was a bright young woman. She kept up on her schoolwork and was self-motivated—at least when it came to reading scriptures, praying, and waking up for seminary. It was harder to feel the same motivation when it came to exercising, eating healthy, and spending less time on her phone. The bishop asked her if she was ready to receive her patriarchal blessing. She had not really thought about it but promised she would speak to her parents. It just seemed like such a big step. Was she ready for this important spiritual milestone when she couldn't even get motivated to make healthy choices? Her mom and dad said they would support her whatever she decided. Still, it seemed like she had a long way to go before she would be completely ready. The next Sunday during the sacrament she felt a prompting: God wasn't waiting for her to be perfect before she took the sacrament. In fact, the sacrament was helping her progress. Wasn't it the same with her patriarchal blessing? Right after the meeting, she quickly approached the bishop. He was smiling. So was she.

In the Church, there are some ages associated with certain events. Members typically get baptized at eight. Children enter Young Women or are ordained to the Aaronic Priesthood the year they turn twelve. Young people typically go on missions around eighteen, nineteen, or twenty. However, that doesn't mean there is an appointed time for everything. The time for receiving a patriarchal blessing is more of a personal decision. You should not feel pressured to get it by—or postpone it until—a certain age. You might ask parents and leaders for advice, but ultimately, it is a decision made between you and Heavenly Father. Some indicators that you are mature enough to receive it are if you have a sincere desire, if you are establishing good spiritual habits like prayer and scripture study, if you have a current temple recommend, and if you recognize your blessings and are setting goals for your future. God has a personal message to reveal to you. As you seek His direction, He will let you know when the best time for you is. President Russell M. Nelson asked, "Does God really *want* to speak to you?" He then answered, "Yes!"[8]

Some hesitate to request their blessings because they feel unworthy. It is important to talk to your parents and bishop about anything that might be worrying you. However, worthiness is not flawlessness. It is honesty with God and priesthood leaders and, with the Lord's help, trying to keep your covenants and learn from mistakes. Ultimate perfection is the long-term goal for after this life. For now, worthiness means making progress in that direction.

Some wonder if their blessings will be affected or limited because they have sinned in the past. Remember that God sees the end from the beginning (see Abraham 2:8). Even when you struggle, He still sees your potential. He is "full of grace and truth" (2 Nephi 2:6). Because He is full of truth, He remembers the faith and spiritual greatness you demonstrated in the premortal existence. He can look beyond current weaknesses, bad habits, and past sins to see your potential. Because God is full of grace, He is willing to help you reach that potential. He can share His vision with you and engage with you in making it a reality.

## PREPARING FOR YOUR BLESSING

Mark had never been much of a fan of general conference. Sitting hour after hour listening to talks wasn't exactly his idea of a good time. His parents expected the family to participate and he didn't fight them. Still, he didn't look forward to it. Then his seminary teacher said, "If you don't get anything out of general conference, it is your own fault." The words struck him. He had never considered that he should do something besides just listen. Mark decided to do better. He looked up a few talks from the previous conference on the Church's website and reviewed them. He also looked up "Prophets, Mission of" in the Topical Guide and was directed to some important scriptures. He had heard he should have a question in mind going into conference. He could not think of a question himself, but he had a friend whose parents were getting divorced and Mark wanted to help him. He determined to listen to see if anyone spoke about how to handle divorces. When conference came, Mark was much more attentive. Instead of distracting himself with his phone, he used it to take notes. No speaker talked directly about divorce, but Mark still found some thoughts that would be perfect to share with his struggling friend. In his next seminary class, the teacher asked students to share something they learned in conference. When Mark's turn came, he said, "I learned that the more you put into it, the more you get out of it."

Mark's lesson also applies to patriarchal blessings. Those who look at the experience as simply a hoop to jump through may not get as much out of it as they could. The fact that you are reading this booklet says a lot about your willingness to prepare or help others prepare.

When the Lord had an important message for Moses, He appeared to him at the burning bush and called his name. He then said, "Put off thy shoes from off thy feet, for the place whereon thou standest is holy ground" (Exodus 3:5). A patriarchal blessing is "precious. It is personal scripture to you."[9] God will call you by name, and you also will be standing—or in this case, sitting—on holy ground. He may not ask you to remove your shoes, but He certainly expects you to remove worldly distractions. Surely, you will be more ready to hear God's message when your mind is not being bombarded with the swear words that fill the lyrics of popular songs. Surely, you will be better prepared when your mind is not full of the violent images included in many electronic games. Surely, you will be better prepared to hear and hearken as you step away from the divisiveness and contention that fill many social media posts.

President Thomas S. Monson wrote, "The same Lord who provided a Liahona for Lehi provides for you and for me today a rare and valuable gift to give direction to our lives. . . . The gift to which I refer is known as your patriarchal blessing."[10] Before Lehi received the Liahona, he left his home and the majority of his possessions in Jerusalem and lived in a tent in the wilderness (see 1 Nephi 2:15). That does not mean you have to go camping before you receive your patriarchal blessing, but it does mean you have to make mindful and conscious efforts to step away from the world.

You might ask parents and leaders what they did or wish they had done to be better prepared for their patriarchal blessings. Your patriarch may also have some suggestions. He may ask you to come with a prayerful attitude and dressed in Sunday attire. Fasting is not required, but you may feel it could help you prepare. Ask him what he does to prepare to give blessings. When you hear how seriously he takes his responsibility, it will help you do the same. Like Mark learned with general conference, the more you put into preparing for your blessing, the more meaningful it will be.

## WHO SHOULD ATTEND?

Bo was a convert. He joined the Church in his twenties and so had not received a patriarchal blessing in his youth. As the day of his blessing approached, he wondered who he should take with him. He knew he could invite his parents and siblings even though they were not Latter-day Saints, but they were still pretty upset about his decision to join the Church. He decided instead to invite his girlfriend. The blessing was amazing, but when Bo and his girlfriend broke up a few weeks later, he regretted sharing such a personal moment with someone who was not going to be a significant part of his life.

Latter-day Saints love to gather to support each other and be supported. Baptisms are typically attended by many family members and friends. Weddings and baby blessings are celebrated in a big way. However, your patriarchal blessing does not call for a reception or party. Nothing should overshadow the sacredness of the experience. Therefore, most patriarchs suggest you bring only your parents or, if you are married, your spouse.

On the day of your blessing, you want to be able to focus, listen intently, and treasure the words being spoken. You may not be able to do that if you are worried about who is there, what they are thinking, or if you are going to be late for the family get-together afterward. Like all deeply spiritual experiences, receiving your blessing should be "harbored and protected and regarded with deepest reverence."[11]

## RECORDING BLESSINGS

When Janice contacted the patriarch to schedule an appointment to receive her blessing, the patriarch complimented her on making this decision and added, "The blessing you receive is so important that it will be recorded and transcribed, and a copy will be preserved in the Church archives." Janice had not realized that before. In fact, she had always heard we are not supposed to record blessings. When she asked the patriarch about it, he said, "It is important to record this blessing so you can read it over and over and it can be a source of comfort and direction throughout your life." He explained that although we do not typically record all blessings, we can record father's blessings. "And, Janice," the patriarch reminded, "this blessing comes directly from your Heavenly Father."

Under the heading "Recording the Words of Ordinances and Blessings" in the Church's *General Handbook* we read, "Patriarchal blessings are recorded and transcribed. The exact wording of other ordinances and blessings is not recorded in writing or by recording device. However, a family may record father's blessings" (38.2.1.5). Other blessings, such as those given during a confirmation, ordination, or setting apart, should not be recorded. It does not mean they are not important. The person receiving the blessing and members of his or her family are encouraged to write in a personal journal the date of the blessing, the name of the one who gave it, and parts of the blessing that were especially meaningful (see 24.8.3, "Setting Apart Missionaries"). You should also write about your patriarchal blessing. Even though you will get a copy, how you felt will not be captured in the transcription. You will find it valuable to write about your feelings, what impressions came to your mind, and what you were aware of before, during, and after the blessing.

Janice found that having a copy of her patriarchal blessing helped her, just as it did another young woman named Laudy. Laudy had the rare opportunity of sharing her testimony in general conference and said, "I have learned to turn to my patriarchal blessing whenever I feel sad or lonely. My blessing helps me to see my potential and the specific plan God has for me. It comforts me and helps me to see beyond my earthly perspective. It reminds me of my gifts and of the blessings I will receive if I live worthily."[12]

## YOUR LINEAGE

Sai's family moved to the United States from India. He grew up as a Hindu but met a young woman at college who introduced him to the Church of Jesus Christ. He enjoyed learning from missionaries and attending Church, but worried that if he became a Christian, he would be turning his back on his family and heritage. Nevertheless, he finally chose to be baptized. After the service, his bishop said, "Sai, I know this was hard for you. I am proud of you. As you were being baptized, I felt such a strong presence. I know your ancestors were watching you with happiness. They are proud of you, too." The bishop's words confirmed that he was not turning his back on his family members. He was doing the most important thing he could ever do for them.[13] Later, when Sai received his patriarchal blessing and was told his lineage, he once again felt the confirmation that his choice to follow Christ and enter a covenant relationship with Him would be a positive turning point for his family—past and future.

When a patriarch puts his hands on your head and declares your lineage, he identifies the tribe through which you will receive your blessings and bless others. However, many people do not know what these tribes are, where they come from, and why they are important.

Remember that God made a covenant with Adam and Eve. As they were obedient, He promised them and their children priesthood power, the fulness of the gospel, sealings, and ultimately eternal life. He later renewed that covenant with Enoch, Noah, and Abraham, who diligently sought after the knowledge and blessings "belonging to the fathers" (Abraham 1:2). The Lord told Abraham that through his seed all the nations of the earth would be blessed (see Genesis 18:18; Abraham 2:9). Because Abraham was so faithful in living the covenant, it started being called the Abrahamic covenant, but it is really the eternal and everlasting covenant God has made with His children in each new dispensation.[14] God renewed the covenant with Abraham's son Isaac (see Genesis 26:1–4, 24), and then with Isaac's son Jacob, who was given a new name: Israel (see Genesis 28:24; 35:9–13).

Thus, Israel is not just a country. It is the name of a man and his descendants. The house of Israel is the family of Jacob. As his sons married, they and their wives became heads of tribes into which many children and grandchildren were born. These tribes formed a strong nation until some turned away from God. Soon enough, they were conquered by foreign powers and most of them were scattered. They intermarried with others and ultimately the blood of this special covenant family was spread throughout the world. In the Book of Mormon, Nephi wrote, "Yea, the more part of all the tribes have been led away" and "scattered upon all the face of the earth, and also among all nations" (1 Nephi 22:4, 3). We speak of most of the descendants of Jacob's family as being lost—not because they do not know where they are, but because they have lost their cultural identities and do not know who they are.[15]

For many people, the history shared above is nothing more than a Bible story, but for Latter-day Saints it is deeply personal. In your patriarchal blessing, you are told your connection with Israel and his sons and daughters. They are your great-great-great-great—many greats—grandparents. Their blood flows in your veins.[16] The words of the Savior to believers in the Book of Mormon apply to you as well: "Ye are the children of the prophets; and ye are of the house of Israel" (3 Nephi 20:25). President Russell M. Nelson said, "You have *inherited* greatness."[17] Sister Julie B. Beck, former Relief

Society General President, said, "You are treasured children of the promise."[18] This means you can choose to make the same covenants ancient prophets made and receive the same promised blessings.

Of course, over the centuries, the bloodlines have been mixed to the point that we all have within us a combination of many bloodlines. This is why President Dallin H. Oaks has taught, "A declaration of lineage is not a scientific pronouncement or an identification of genetic inheritance."[19] Patriarchs identify lineage "by the promptings of the Holy Ghost . . . regardless of the race or nationality of the person receiving the blessing."[20] People within the same family—even identical twins—can be named from different tribes, because a patriarchal blessing is not a physical DNA test. Instead, it "reminds you," as President Russell M. Nelson explained, "of your linkage with the past. And it will help you realize your future potential."[21] Being born in this family means you have been given temporal and spiritual blessings with the hope and expectation that you will use them to help all God's children.

Because God loves all His children, He sent us to earth. He wanted us to learn and grow, but also to come safely back to Him. That is why He looked among His children and found some faithful whom He could trust. To those He gave extra responsibilities. Your lineage means you were and are part of this faithful, trusted group.

In preparation for the Savior's return, God started gathering these trusted gatherers. He brought forth the Book of Mormon, the instrument of gathering,[22] and restored the gospel again in its fulness. He sent Moses to give Joseph Smith the keys of the gathering of Israel (see D&C 110:11). The very prophet who had once brought the children of Israel out of the slavery of Egypt had come again to bring them out of a different kind of slavery: the slavery of ignorance.

The gathering began with only a few initially, but now the work is spreading throughout the world. Currently the responsibilities of those from Ephraim, Manasseh, Reuben, Levi, Judah, Dan, Naphtali, Benjamin, and all the rest are similar. All the tribes are working together to prepare for the Second Coming. However, when Jesus comes to rule and reign, your tribe will matter a great deal. At that point, each tribe will be given specific responsibilities and assignments. You may see symbolic hints about these future assignments in Israel's blessings to his sons (see Genesis 49:1–28) and Moses's blessings for the tribes (see Deuteronomy 33). You may also be taught "here a little and there a little" (2 Nephi 28:30) by the Spirit about your lineage as your life unfolds. Still, you may not fully understand why you were designated from a certain tribe until the Millennium. President Dallin H. Oaks said your declaration of lineage is important as it "concerns the government of the kingdom of God."[23] Knowing our tribes *now* gives the Lord an additional level of worldwide organization He can call into action when the time comes.

When Christ comes again, billions of people will immediately want to learn about Him and His Church. Little wonder the scriptures say it will be in the Millennium that the gathering of Israel will "commence" in earnest (see 3 Nephi 21:24–28). However, if we wait until that moment to get organized, it will be too late. We need to have strong and experienced leaders already in place throughout the world, not only to handle the dramatic growth of the Church but also the additional temporal responsibilities that will be ours when "the government shall be upon [Christ's] shoulder" (Isaiah 9:6). Every tribe is important. Elder LeGrand Richards said, "Promises of the Lord unto Abraham, Isaac, and Jacob, will not be realized through any one branch of the house of Israel, but through all of them."[24]

The name *Israel* means "Let God prevail" (Bible Dictionary, 708). President Russell M. Nelson reminded the Church of that definition and asked, "Are *you* willing to let God prevail in your life? Are *you* willing to let God be the most important influence in your life?"[25] You have been trusted to make that choice for yourself and ensure that everyone has the opportunity to make the same choice. As you strive to *live* the gospel, *care* for those in need, *invite* others to receive the gospel, and *unite* families for eternity in temples, you are gathering Israel and preparing for the Second Coming. You are inviting all who will to come unto Christ and receive the blessings of His Atonement. This work is vital, but it is not an end in and of itself. Our task is not to gather everyone into the house of Israel, but to ultimately gather all God's children home to Him. Your lineage means you were sent to earth with an important part to play in this great work.

## SHARING YOUR BLESSING

Ruth was asked to speak in sacrament meeting, and the topic she was assigned reminded her of a part in her patriarchal blessing. She asked her mom if she thought she should share it. Ruth's mom was hesitant to tell her she did not think it was a good idea and risk dampening her daughter's efforts to prepare her talk. Instead she said, "Well, God gave you that blessing. Why don't you ask Him whether you should share it?" That night when she prayed, Ruth did as her mother suggested. The next morning, she decided it would be better to share a personal experience she'd had at girls' camp instead of a portion of her blessing.

Ruth had not read the Church's *General Handbook*, but the Spirit gave her the same instruction: "Each patriarchal blessing is sacred, confidential, and personal. . . . Church members should not compare blessings and should not share them except with close family members. Patriarchal blessings should not be read in Church meetings or other public gatherings" (18.17.1, "Receiving a Patriarchal Blessing"). It may sometimes be appropriate to allude to a few words or a main point, but be careful to not share an entire outline or long quotes.

President Boyd K. Packer wrote, "I have learned that strong, impressive spiritual experiences do not come to us very frequently. And when they do, they are generally for our own edification, instruction, or correction." The same is certainly true about our patriarchal blessings. President Packer continued, "I have come to believe also that it is not wise to continually talk of unusual spiritual experiences. They are to be guarded with care and shared only when the Spirit itself prompts you to use them. . . . We are, I believe, to keep these things and ponder them in our hearts."[26]

You live in a world immersed in social media on which people share pictures, information, and experiences so openly that it is sometimes hard to know where to draw the line. Some people learn the hard way that once something is shared, it is out there forever. Patriarchal blessings are not secret, but they are personal and sacred. They should be guarded and protected.

## STUDYING YOUR BLESSING

Ann wanted to give her husband David something special for Valentine's Day. After nearly fifty years of marriage, they had given each other many gifts, but she wanted this one to be different. She had the impression to read his patriarchal blessing and look up the scriptural foundation for the phrases, concepts, and counsel he had been given. Ann and David had read their blessings together before, but they had never really studied them in this way. Through her efforts she discovered something incredible. She found over forty related scriptures! They were a spiritual revelation about her husband, but also related to her own patriarchal blessing. When she finally presented the document to her husband, he was amazed. They read through it together and were struck with how consistently Heavenly Father teaches truth in both blessings and the scriptures. The words may be different, but the intent is the same. "Seek, and ye shall find" (Matthew 7:7) became the theme of that special Valentine's gift.[27]

Elder David A. Bednar explained that we can improve our scripture study by looking for relationships and links between ideas. He said, "Prayerfully identifying, learning about, and pondering such connections . . . is a primary source of living water and yields inspired insights and treasures of hidden knowledge."[28] Elder Bednar did not speak of including patriarchal blessings, but Ann and her husband definitely found treasured insights as they did.

Once, I was traveling home on an airplane and the man next to me asked what I was reading. I answered, "The Book of Mormon."

Seeing that my copy was quite worn, he inquired, "How many times have you read it?"

"Many times," I responded.

He said, "Well, I think it is better to read a hundred books once than the same book one hundred times."

I explained, "Not when it comes to *this* book. Every time I read it, I learn something new."

When Nephi described the Liahona that guided his family to the promised land, he spoke of "a new writing, which was plain to be read" that appeared on the pointers to give "understanding concerning the ways of the Lord; and it was written and changed from time to time" (1 Nephi 16:29). Elder Robert E. Wells, emeritus General Authority Seventy, wrote, "I can find no further reference to this changeable writing. As I read the Book of Mormon, however, something strange seems to happen to me. Passages of scriptures that I have read many times in one light seem to change—and suddenly there is a new meaning to that old and familiar scripture. . . . If we are interested enough to read it again and again, from cover to cover, there are times when a 'new writing'—plain to be read—seems to appear."[29]

Your patriarchal blessing functions the same way. At one point in your life, a certain phrase might stick out. Later, another sentence will become significant. As the circumstances of your life change, you might notice ideas and promises in your blessing to which you never paid much attention before. Specific words that may not have ever seemed especially meaningful can take on great importance in a new phase of your life. That is why it is essential to read your blessing not just once, but often throughout your life.

Some people want to set up a meeting and talk to the patriarch who gave their blessings to find out more about what he was thinking or feeling at the time. They think he can interpret the words he was given. Patriarchs will kindly tell these people that neither patriarchs nor bishops should interpret blessings.[30] Your blessing is not about the relationship between you and your patriarch or bishop, but between you and God. When you seek greater understanding, go directly to Heavenly Father in prayer for the answers and explanations you desire. As you are faithful to your covenants, He will reveal more throughout your life. The Lord has said, "For unto him that receiveth I will give more" (2 Nephi 28:30).

## APPLYING YOUR BLESSING

When Katina left her native land of Russia to attend Brigham Young University, she took a copy of her patriarchal blessing with her. When she moved from the dorms to an apartment, she misplaced her blessing. Her parents could not easily send her a copy, so Katina was happy when her bishop told her she could view and print another copy by signing in on the Church's website and clicking on "Patriarchal Blessing." She was glad she had access to it again, because now she desired to do something besides read it. She was at a crossroads and making a lot of decisions that would affect her future. She needed to apply her blessing in her life.

Applying your blessing means allowing it to inform your choices and make a difference. It can help you count blessings, set goals, and find heroes. When, like Katina, you are at a crossroads, you might ask yourself, "What am I thankful for in my past, and how do my future plans align with my patriarchal blessing? Should I keep going or make some adjustments based on direction I have been given?" The Children and Youth program encourages you to strive to grow as Jesus did: "In wisdom and stature, and in favour with God and man" (Luke 2:52). You might ask yourself, "What intellectual, physical, spiritual, and social goals can I set based on my patriarchal blessing?" Your blessing may mention positive attributes, talents, and characteristics God wants you to recognize and develop. Try asking, "Who is someone I look up to because he or she has developed those same traits?" Let those people become heroes to you.

Peter Vidmar, a Latter-day Saint gymnast who won multiple gold medals at the 1984 Olympics, received his patriarchal blessing when he was nineteen and used it to set goals in every aspect of his life. His blessing spoke of gymnastics (physical), but also of the importance of education (intellectual). It counseled him to be kind to others (social) and stay close to Heavenly Father (spiritual).

His blessing also helped him find heroes as it pointed him toward his ancestors. His dad dealt with polio but never let it stop him. His mom was always punctual and taught Peter to keep his commitments. One of his grandfathers was an orphan who sacrificed greatly to give his children the formal education he'd never had. One of his great-great-grandfathers was Solomon Chamberlain, who had a vision that the Church of Jesus Christ would be restored, and he lived to see that day. Solomon met Hyrum and Joseph Smith, joined the Church, and became one of its earliest missionaries.[31]

Did you know that if your own ancestors were members of the Church, you can view and print copies of their patriarchal blessings? You can request the blessings of deceased relatives from the Church's website. Sign into your account, click on "Patriarchal Blessing," and click again on "Request Family Blessing." You will need to provide some names, birthdays, and explain your relationship, but you can be given access to read their blessings. You may come to realize that just as the blessings given to Israel's sons and daughters in the Old Testament apply to you (see Genesis 49), the blessings given to other ancestors can be meaningful as well. As you read their blessings, you can imagine them and other ancestors pulling for your success from the other side of the veil, for surely they are doing just that.

Applying your patriarchal blessing means to "look forward with an eye of faith" (Alma 5:15). When Alma said those words, he was teaching people who lived long before Christ, and yet he told them to view themselves with resurrected bodies standing before God. These events would not happen for many years, but Alma taught them to picture the future as if it had already happened. Similarly, Lehi said, "I have obtained a land of promise" long before he actually did (1 Nephi 5:5). Can you picture the fulfillment of your plans and goals as if they already happened? Can you picture yourself as if you already had the characteristics you desire? You might try writing a journal page as if it were a year, five years, or ten years from now. Setting and reaching goals and emulating worthy heroes is learning to exercise faith in Christ.[32]

## WHAT IF?

My wife Debi did not receive her patriarchal blessing until she left home to attend a university. When she obtained her recommend and called the patriarch to set an appointment, she wondered how this man would be able to give her a meaningful blessing when he knew nothing about her. Still, she had faith that the blessing was not coming from him. That truth has been confirmed to Debi many times as the years have passed and the promises in her blessing have been fulfilled in remarkable ways.

Debi's experience is not uncommon. Many in the Church testify of how personal and special their blessings are—even when the patriarch did not know them well. Nevertheless, there are others who question, "What if he tells me to pursue something and I don't want to?" or "What if the patriarch says something that does not happen?"

Patriarchal blessings are not unalterable decrees. You are not a chess piece being moved around a board by a God who has predestined you to certain things at certain times—like it or not. Your life is not scripted so meticulously that you have no choice. You have agency, and God expects you to use it.

Along with personal choice, the fulfillment of your blessing is also dependent upon your faithfulness. When Nephi described the Liahona, he said it worked "according to the faith and diligence and heed" of Lehi and his family (1 Nephi 16:28). Patriarchal blessings are similar.

In addition to personal choice and faithfulness, promised blessings are dependent on God's timing. One young man was concerned because his brother received his patriarchal blessing and then died in a tragic car accident. He asked his father, "Why did God promise he would serve a mission and marry but then he died?"

With great faith, his father testified, "He is still alive. God has an eternal perspective, and your brother will still have those opportunities." Indeed, according to our faith and righteous desires, the promised blessings can be fulfilled "in this life and in eternity" (*General Handbook*, 18.17.1, "Receiving a Patriarchal Blessing").

We read in Alma 34:32 that "this life is the time for men to prepare to meet God; yea, behold the day of this life is the day for men to perform their labors." However, we sometimes forget that the spirit world is a continuation of the probationary period that is this life.[33] President Dallin H. Oaks taught, "Our progress need not conclude with the end of mortality."[34] This doctrine makes even more sense when we remember that Brigham Young taught that the spirit world is another dimension right on this earth.[35]

Elder Neal A. Maxwell wrote, "We tend to overlook the reality that the spirit world . . . [is] part, really, of the second estate. The work of the Lord, so far as the second estate is concerned, is completed before the Judgment and Resurrection. . . . Our existence in the spirit world is part of the mortal sector of our Father's plan. . . . [God] provides in the spirit world a continuum of mortality's probation, the great opportunity for all."[36]

What if someone dies before she or he receives a patriarchal blessing? What if a blessing speaks of callings that never come? What if a blessing speaks of fulfilling a mission and then the missionary comes home early due to health issues? What if a young woman is told she will be married in the temple and she never marries? The list of questions can go on and on.[37] General answers often fall short when addressing such specific and personal circumstances. Nevertheless, as you strive to keep an eternal perspective, you can trust that no blessing will be out of reach. Elder John A. Widtsoe said, "It should always be kept in mind that the realization of the promises made may come in this or the future life. [Members] have stumbled at times because promised blessings have not occurred in this life. They have failed to remember that, in the gospel, life with all its activities continues forever and that the labors of earth may be continued in heaven."[38]

## IMMORTALITY AND ETERNAL LIFE

President Russell M. Nelson was once asked what he desired for the youth of the Church. He said, "They need an eternal perspective." He explained, "When Joseph Smith was in the Liberty Jail, he felt abandoned and discouraged. He poured his heart out to

God, and was told, 'All these things shall give thee experience, and shall be for thy good' (D&C 122:7). God did not change Joseph's circumstances. He changed his perspective, and that changed everything!"[39]

Your patriarchal blessing is about the big picture. God doesn't want you so focused on a puzzle piece that you miss the whole puzzle. He doesn't want you so bogged down getting through each day that you miss the entire purpose of your life.

God's work and glory is to "bring to pass the immortality and eternal life" of His children (Moses 1:39). Because of the Atonement of Jesus Christ, you will be resurrected and live forever. That is immortality. You also have the chance to live forever with your family and God. That is eternal life. Paul wrote, "Eye hath not seen, nor ear heard, neither have entered into the heart of man, the things which God hath prepared for them that love him" (1 Corinthians 2:9). That is some big joy and big purpose, and it is possible for all of us.

Your patriarchal blessing is but a prelude to receiving even greater blessings from your Father. The Lord said, "For he that receiveth my servants [including the patriarch who has been called and set apart] receiveth me; And he that receiveth me receiveth my Father; And he that receiveth my Father receiveth my Father's kingdom; therefore all that my Father hath shall be given unto him" (D&C 84:36–38).

All that the Father has is hard to imagine, but your patriarchal blessing isn't just about what you will get. It is about what you can become through the grace of God and Christ. God is not just preparing a mansion in heaven for you (see John 14:2), but He is also preparing you for the mansion. Along with preparing thrones and kingdoms for you (see D&C 132:19), God is also preparing you to become a king or a queen ready to sit in those thrones and govern those kingdoms in righteousness. Not only can you live *with* your Heavenly Parents, but you can live *like* Them—create like Them, love and serve like Them, and parent like Them. There is no greater happiness and joy (see Abraham 1:2), no greater gift (see D&C 6:13), and no greater blessing.

# NOTES

1. Neal A. Maxwell, "A More Determined Discipleship," *Ensign*, February 1979, 70.
2. Thomas S. Monson, "Your Patriarchal Blessing: A Liahona of Light," *Ensign*, November 1986, 65.
3. Special thanks to Keith J. Wilson and Michael R. Kelly, two friends who are patriarchs and were willing to review this booklet and offer valuable input.
4. Neal A. Maxwell, "Free to Choose" (Brigham Young University devotional, March 16, 2004), 5, speeches.byu.edu.
5. Wendy W. Nelson, "Hope of Israel," supplement to the *New Era* and *Ensign*, August 2018, 4, 6; italics in original.
6. See Neal A. Maxwell, *Even as I Am* (Salt Lake City: Deseret Book, 1982), 93.
7. Spencer W. Kimball, "The Role of Righteous Women," *Ensign*, November 1979, 102.
8. Russell M. Nelson, "Revelation for the Church, Revelation for Our Lives," *Ensign*, May 2018, 95; italics in original.
9. Russell M. Nelson, "Thanks for the Covenant" (Brigham Young University devotional, November 22, 1988), 5, speeches.byu.edu.
10. Thomas S. Monson, "Your Patriarchal Blessing: A Liahona of Light," *Ensign*, November 1986, 65.
11. Boyd K. Packer, *Teach Ye Diligently* (Salt Lake City: Deseret Book, 1975), 71.
12. Laudy Kaouk, "How the Priesthood Blesses Youth," *Ensign*, May 2020, 56.
13. For a more detailed account of Sai's story, see Brad Wilcox, *Because of the Christ on Calvary* (Salt Lake City: Deseret Book, 2020), 12–15.
14. See Robert J. Matthews, "Our Covenants with the Lord," *Ensign*, December 1980, 35–36.
15. See Jeffrey R. Chadwick, "Review of Zvi Ben-Dor Benite's *The Ten Lost Tribes: A World History*" (New York: Oxford University Press, 2009), *BYU Studies Quarterly* 53, no. 1 (2014), 183–84.
16. See Joseph Fielding Smith, *Doctrines of Salvation*, comp. Bruce R. McConkie, 3 vols. (Salt Lake City: Bookcraft, 1999), 3:249; rare exceptions are "grafted into the house of Israel."
17. Russell M. Nelson, "Thanks for the Covenant," 7; italics added.
18. Julie B. Beck, "You Have a Noble Birthright," *Ensign*, May 2006, 107.

# NOTES

19. Dallin H. Oaks, "Patriarchal Blessings," *Worldwide Leadership Training Meeting: The Patriarch* (Salt Lake City: The Church of Jesus Christ of Latter-day Saints, January 8, 2005), 8.
20. Dallin H. Oaks, Information and Suggestions for Patriarchs (Salt Lake City: The Church of Jesus Christ of Latter-day Saints, n. d.), as quoted by Daniel H. Ludlow, *Selected Writings of Daniel H. Ludlow* (Salt Lake City: Deseret Book, 2000), 528.
21. Russell M. Nelson, "Thanks for the Covenant," 5.
22. See Ezra Taft Benson, "Flooding the Earth with the Book of Mormon," *Ensign*, November 1988, 4.
23. Dallin H. Oaks, "Patriarchal Blessings," 8.
24. LeGrand Richards, *Israel! Do You Know?* (Salt Lake City: Deseret Book, 1954), 8.
25. Russell M. Nelson, "Let God Prevail," *Ensign*, November 2020, 94; italics in original.
26. Boyd K. Packer, "The Candle of the Lord," *Ensign*, January 1983, 53.
27. Thanks to good friends Ann and David Seamons, who allowed me to share this experience.
28. David A. Bednar, "A Reservoir of Living Water" (Brigham Young University devotional, February 4, 2007), 4, speeches.byu.edu.
29. Robert E. Wells, "The Liahona Triad," in *The Book of Mormon Treasury: Gospel Insights from General Authorities and Religious Educators* (Salt Lake City: Deseret Book, 2003), 93–94.
30. See Boyd K. Packer, "The Stake Patriarch," *Ensign*, November 2002, 43.
31. See Larry C. Porter, "Solomon Chamberlain—Early Missionary," *BYU Studies* 12, no. 3 (1972), 314–17.
32. I appreciate Brother Ahmad S. Corbitt for sharing this insight; see also *Preach My Gospel: A Guide to Missionary Service* (2004), 146, 152.
33. See Mark A. Mathews, "'Between the Time of Death and the Resurrection': A Doctrinal Examination of the Spirit World," *Religious Educator*, vol. 21, no. 1, 2020, 105–31.
34. Dallin H. Oaks, "The Great Plan," *Ensign*, May 2020, 95.
35. See *Discourses of Brigham Young*, comp. John A. Widtsoe (Salt Lake City: Bookcraft, 1998), 376.
36. Neal A. Maxwell, *The Promise of Discipleship* (Salt Lake City: Deseret Book, 2001), 111–14.
37. See Alonzo L. Gaskill, *65 Questions and Answers about Patriarchal Blessings* (Springville, UT: CFI, 2018), 27–29.
38. John A. Widtsoe, *Evidences and Reconciliations* (Salt Lake City: Bookcraft, 1960), 323.
39. Personal communication in a meeting with the Young Men General Presidency, August 11, 2020.